Harriet Quimby
A Woman of Firsts

by Paul Daniels

AF251266

Harriet, the Writer

On that December day in 1903, when the Wright brothers made that first historic flight, hardly anyone knew about it. Soon, though, the newspapers were full of stories about this exciting development in flight.

Over the next several years, airplanes were improved. The Wright brothers and others started flight schools to teach people how to fly. Pilots around the country drummed up interest in flying. Air shows and races thrilled crowds that came to watch. One of those watching was a woman named Harriet Quimby. Before long, Harriet would make a name for herself as one of the most daring pilots in the country.

No one knows for sure when Harriet Quimby was born. It might have been May 1, 1875. She grew up in Michigan. When she was twenty-five, she moved to California. There Harriet began her career as a writer. She wrote about life in and around San Francisco. She wrote about art and artists. She wrote reviews of plays she saw in the theater. Her writing was interesting and lively, and people enjoyed what she wrote.

After three years in California, Harriet was ready for a bigger market for her work. She moved across the country to New York.

Before long, she began writing for a newspaper called *Leslie's Illustrated Weekly*. She wrote theater reviews as well as columns for women. She told women how to manage money, fix their own cars, find a job, and other things of interest to them. She also visited Cuba, Egypt, and other countries. She wrote about all these fascinating places and the interesting people she met.

In 1906, Harriet's newspaper sent her to cover an automobile race. She didn't just watch the race from the stands. She got in one of the cars and raced around the track. The ride thrilled her, and she wrote a dazzling article about it.

Harriet, the Pilot

Four years later, Harriet was at the Belmont Racetrack in New York. Horses usually raced there. On this day, Harriet was there to watch a different kind of race. This was an air race that would go around the Statue of Liberty. One of the men flying was a well-known pilot named John Moisant. He was flying for the United States in the race. He became even more famous that day because he won the race.

Harriet met John Moisant and his sister, Matilde. By the time the race was over and the group disbanded, Harriet and Matilde were fast friends. Both of them were also keen on flying.

Harriet and Matilde decided to take flying lessons. The Wright brothers had a flight school, but they refused to teach women. In those days, many people believed that women belonged in the home. The idea of women pilots was fairly shocking to most.

Harriet and Matilde were determined to fly in spite of the pressure society exerted on them to act like "ladies." They could not learn to fly from the Wright brothers, but they did know of another school they could try. Matilde's brothers, John and Alfred, owned a flying school. John agreed to teach them how to fly.

In May 1911, Harriet and Matilde began attending flight school. They went to classes to learn how to get an airplane off the ground. They learned how to stabilize an airplane. In addition to their classroom studies, the two friends climbed into airplanes and began learning how to fly.

At first, no one knew that Harriet was taking flying lessons. When word slipped out, her story was big news. Soon she was writing columns about her astounding experiences learning how to fly.

On the last day of July, she began taking her pilot's license tests. She took off and flew well, but her landing was not so great. She did not pass, but she was told she could try again the next day. On August 1, 1911, she took off again. This time her landing was perfect. Harriet Quimby became the first American woman to earn her pilot's license. She was also only the second woman in the world who had earned one.

Harriet loved flying. She also loved breaking records. On the night of September 4, Harriet made another first for a woman. She flew at night. Photographers snapped her picture. Reporters wrote stories about her. Harriet had rigged her own purple satin flying costume with a hood. Hers was not a replica of the long coat and cap that male pilots used. She was one of a kind, and the public loved her.

Two months later, Harriet and Matilde headed south of the United States, to Mexico. They were part of the flying show that the Moisant brothers were putting on. When Harriet flew over the crowds there, she set another record. She became the first woman to pilot a plane over Mexico City.

Harriet, the Hero

When the air show was over, Matilde went on to fly in other shows with her brothers' team. Harriet had other schemes she wanted to check out. Two years earlier, a man named Louis Bleriot had become the first person to fly a plane across the English Channel. Harriet wanted to be the first woman to do the same. Bleriot had flown from France to England. She would fly from England to France.

This would not be an easy record to break.
The English Channel was well-known for its fast
changing weather. From October through April,
the weather was often terrible. It got cold and
rainy, and in an open airplane, pilots would
be soaked and chilled. The fog could make it
impossible for pilots to see where they were going.
Strong winds could push a plane off course or into
the sea below.

In March 1912, Harriet sailed to England. She borrowed a plane from Louis Bleriot and made her final plans for her record flight. Few people knew about Harriet's plans to cross the English Channel. She had kept her plans secret because she didn't want another woman to break the record before her.

One person she did trust with her secret was another pilot, Gustav Hamel. He was afraid for Harriet's life. He offered to dress in Harriet's purple satin flying costume and fly the plane across the English Channel himself. Then Harriet could meet him when he landed and pretend that she had flown the plane across herself. Harriet would have no part of that lie. She would fly across the English Channel herself—or die trying.

On the morning of April 16, 1912, Harriet Quimby took off from Dover on the English coast. Clouds filled the sky, and Harriet flew inside the clouds almost all the way across the channel. She could barely see where she was headed. Then, fifty-nine minutes later, she landed on a beach in northern France.

She had done it! Harriet Quimby had become the first woman to fly across the English Channel. She had shown that with enough determination and experience, she could follow her dreams and do what others thought impossible for a woman to do.

Think Critically

1. Draw a time line of important events in Harriet Quimby's life from 1910 through 1912.

2. Why didn't Harriet Quimby learn to fly from the Wright brothers?

3. What do you think was Harriet Quimby's opinion about the beliefs of what women should and shouldn't do? Explain your answer.

4. Would you like to have had Harriet Quimby for a friend? Explain why or why not.

5. How can you tell that Harriet Quimby was a competitive person?

 **Science**

Learn about the English Channel Find out more about the English Channel by doing research on the Internet or going to the library. Why is it called the English Channel? What is the weather like there? Is it salt water or fresh water? Take notes to record your findings.

School-Home Connection Explain to family members who Harriet Quimby was and why people still remember her.

Word Count: 1,180

Babe Didrikson Zaharias

The World's Greatest Athlete

by Barbara A. Donovan

Some say she was the greatest woman athlete of all time. Some say she was the greatest athlete of all time— man or woman. In 1950, the Associated Press voted her the world's greatest woman athlete since 1900. In 1932, 1945, 1946, 1947, 1950, and 1954, the Associated Press named her Woman Athlete of the Year. No man or woman had ever earned this honor of Athlete of the Year six times. No one has done it since then either.

Who was this wonder woman? Her name was Babe Didrikson Zaharias. She was a woman who practiced long and hard to soar to the top of each sport she tried.

When Babe was born on June 26, 1914, her parents named her Mildred Ella. Some stories say that she got the name Babe when she was growing up. This was because she could hit home runs over the fence just like the famous Babe Ruth. However she got her name, Babe was a talented athlete from the very beginning.

Babe grew up in Beaumont, Texas. Her family did not live in luxury. As long as there was a sport to play and kids to play with, Babe was happy. When teams were picked for a sport, she was always one of the first players chosen. However, she was not well liked. She often didn't get along with the other children. She had an intense desire to win at every sport she played. By the time she was in her teens, Babe knew what she wanted out of life. She wanted to be the greatest athlete ever. Babe would not "fumble" that dream for anything.

In the years when Babe was growing up, many people believed that only a few sports were appropriate for girls to play. Babe didn't pay any attention to what others thought. She played whatever sport she wanted, even if she was the only girl on the team. She was such a talented athlete. Most boys had no problem adding Babe to their teams.

One of the sports that girls did play at that time was basketball. Babe quickly became the star of her high school team. In 1930, Babe got an offer to work as an assistant at a Dallas insurance company before she finished high school. The company didn't want Babe because they thought she'd make a great assistant. They wanted her to play on the company's basketball team. It was called the Golden Cyclones. In those days, women's basketball teams run by churches or corporations were very popular. From 1930–1932, Babe played basketball for the Golden Cyclones. In each of those three years, Babe was named to the All-American women's basketball team. In 1931, she led her team to the national championship.

At the same time, Babe started running and jumping in track and field events. The company she worked for had a track team, too, so she joined that team. It did not come as a surprise that Babe was a track star, too. By 1932, the American, Olympic, and world records in five different track and field events were hers.

In 1932, Babe entered the national amateur track meet for women. Babe was the only member of the Golden Cyclones team to enter. Her competition was a team from the Illinois Women's Athletic Club. It had twenty team members.

To the astonishment of everyone, the one-woman team of Babe Didrikson defeated all the other teams in the event. She had won six gold medals along the way. She had also broken four world records along the way. By herself, Babe earned thirty points. The second-place team from Illinois earned only twenty-two points. The triumphant Babe was featured in newspapers around the country. Babe was famous, and she was headed for the Olympic Games.

Babe went to Los Angeles, California, for the 1932 Summer Olympic Games. Once again, Babe showed that she was a winner. Her javelin throw (an event where a person throws a spear-like object) of 143 feet 4 inches (43.7 m) set an Olympic record. It also won Babe her first gold medal. Then Babe propelled herself over the 80-meter (262.5 ft.) hurdles in 11.7 seconds. With that time, she set an Olympic record. It won her another gold medal.

Finally, Babe jumped 5 feet 5 1/4 inches (1.7 m) in the high jump. This is an event where athletes must jump over a horizontal bar. That distance should have tied for first place. Instead she earned the silver medal for second place because she was penalized. That was because when she lunged forward, her head went over the bar first. That way of jumping was not yet allowed. Now it has become the way it is done.

Babe was a hero. At the end of 1932, she was voted Woman Athlete of the Year for the first time. After holding amateur status for many years, Babe turned professional in late 1932. That meant she could begin earning money for playing sports. She could also appear in advertisements.

Struggling to make a good living as a professional athlete, she played in an exhibition basketball game in New York. In 1933, she played with a professional basketball team called Babe Didrikson's All-Americans. The tour was successful for several years. In 1934, Babe went to Florida and was paid to pitch in major league exhibition baseball games during spring training. As a result of her hard work, Babe was able to earn the money she needed.

Then Babe started playing golf. She practiced hard.
She would hit more than a thousand balls in a day.
She'd swing her golf club until her hands started to
bleed. She won her first tournament in 1935.

Then the
United States Golf
Association (USGA)
made a decision
that hurt Babe.
Since she was a
professional in one
sport, they said she
was a professional
in golf, too. As a
result, she could
no longer play in
most of the golf
tournaments open
to women. Very few
of them were open
to professionals.

In 1938, Babe married a wrestler named George Zaharias. Her husband had money, so Babe no longer needed to play professional sports. She knew that if she sat out a certain amount of time, then she could become an amateur again. Babe decided to do it. The timing turned out to be perfect. Because of World War II, there were no golf tournaments. Finally, in 1943, the USGA said that Babe had waited long enough. She was considered an amateur again. Babe started to play golf in earnest. She never looked back.

Babe played golf so well that, in 1945, she earned her second Woman Athlete of the Year award. Then, she won it again after winning a record-breaking thirteen tournaments in a row in the 1946-47 season. One of these tournaments was the British Women's Amateur tournament. Babe was the first American woman to ever win that title.

In 1947, Babe decided to become a professional golfer once again. Women could earn very little money playing golf in those days. To help the sport, Babe joined with some other people to start the LPGA—the Ladies Professional Golf Association. In 1950, there were only three major professional golf tournaments for women. Babe won all three of them.

In 1953, Babe found out that she had cancer. Even that didn't stop her. The following year, while being treated for the disease, she won five more tournaments. Sadly, none of the remedies she tried made her well. In 1956, Babe Didrikson Zaharias died.

Babe had won ten major golf tournaments. Since then, only three women have won more majors than Babe did. Babe set Olympic and world records in track and field. She showed that a woman could be anything she wanted to be—including a world-class athlete.

Think Critically

1. As a child, why didn't the other children like Babe?

2. Based on the information in the book, draw a time line that includes five key events in Babe's life.

3. How was Babe like many athletes of today? How was she different?

4. Do you think that Babe lived up to her teenage ambition to be the greatest athlete in the world? Explain your answer.

5. What do you think it takes to become a champion athlete like Babe?

 **Social Studies**

Fact Find Use an encyclopedia, the Internet, or another nonfiction book to find information about the history of the Ladies Professional Golf Association. Write a paragraph on your findings.

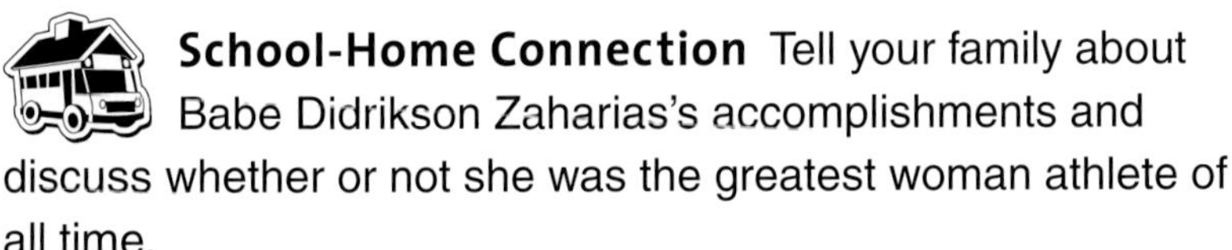 **School-Home Connection** Tell your family about Babe Didrikson Zaharias's accomplishments and discuss whether or not she was the greatest woman athlete of all time.

Word Count: 1,297